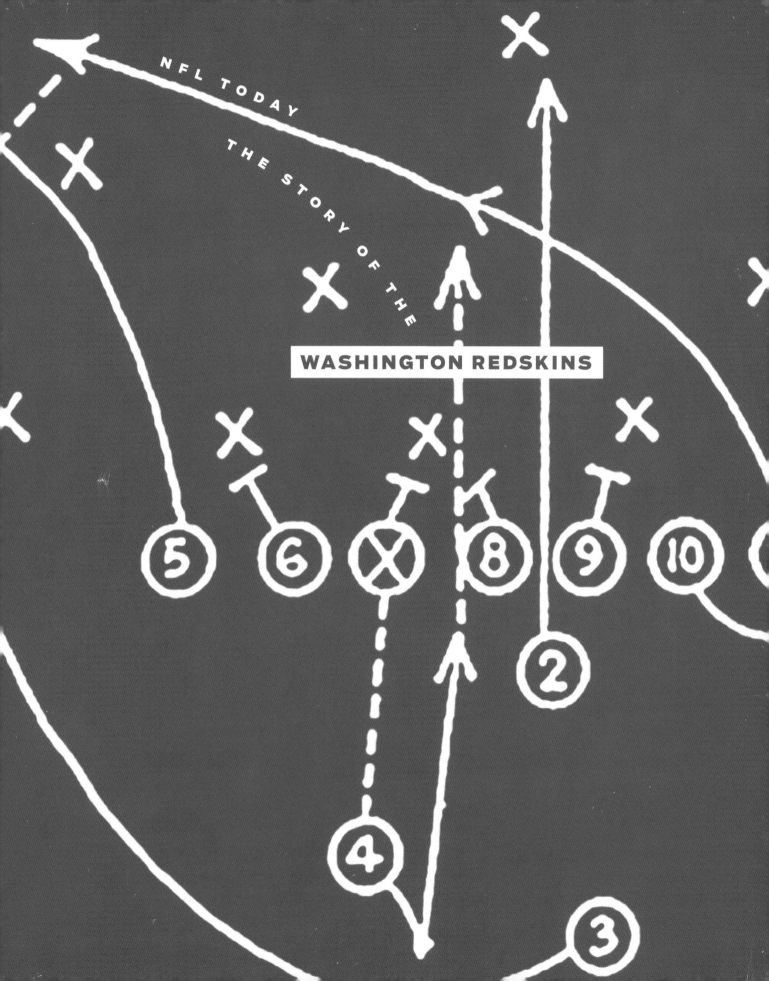

NFL TODAY

THE STORY OF THE

WASHINGTON REDSKINS

NFL TODAY

THE STORY OF THE WASHINGTON REDSKINS

SARA GILBERT

CREATIVE EDUCATION

PUBLISHED BY CREATIVE EDUCATION
P.O. BOX 227, MANKATO, MINNESOTA 56002
CREATIVE EDUCATION IS AN IMPRINT OF THE CREATIVE COMPANY
WWW.THECREATIVECOMPANY.US

DESIGN AND PRODUCTION BY BLUE DESIGN
ART DIRECTION BY RITA MARSHALL
PRINTED IN THE UNITED STATES OF AMERICA

PHOTOGRAPHS BY CORBIS (WALLY MCNAMEE), GETTY IMAGES (ROBERT BECK/SPORTS ILLUSTRATED, AL BELLO, BRUCE BENNETT STUDIOS, BERNSTEIN ASSOCIATES, ROB CARR, MARK CUNNINGHAM, STEVE DESLICH/MCT, NATE FINE/NFL, MARK GAIL/MCT, FOCUS ON SPORT, JED JACOBSOHN, G. NEWMAN LOWRANCE, JOHN MCDONNELL/WASHINGTON POST, JIM MCISAAC, AL MESSERSCHMIDT, TOM MIHALEK/AFP, JONATHAN NEWTON/WASHINGTON POST, NFL, BOB PETERSON/TIME & LIFE PICTURES, PHOTOPIX, PRO FOOTBALL HALL OF FAME/NFL, PAUL SPINELLI, ALLEN DEAN STEELE/NFL, RICK STEWART, DAVID STLUKA, SHAWN THEW/AFP, ROB TRINGALI/ SPORTSCHROME, HARRY WALKER/MCT, JEFF ZELEVANSKY)

LIBRARY OF CONGRESS CATALOGING-IN-PUBLICATION DATA
GILBERT, SARA.
THE STORY OF THE WASHINGTON REDSKINS / SARA GILBERT.
P. CM. — (NFL TODAY)
INCLUDES INDEX.
SUMMARY: THE HISTORY OF THE NATIONAL FOOTBALL LEAGUE'S WASHINGTON REDSKINS, SURVEYING THE FRANCHISE'S BIGGEST STARS AND MOST MEMORABLE MOMENTS FROM ITS INAUGURAL SEASON IN 1932 TO TODAY.
ISBN 978-1-60818-323-4
1. WASHINGTON REDSKINS (FOOTBALL TEAM)—HISTORY—JUVENILE LITERATURE. I. TITLE.

GV956.W3G55 2013
796.332'6409753—DC23   2012033821

FIRST EDITION
9 8 7 6 5 4 3 2 1

COVER: QUARTERBACK ROBERT GRIFFIN III
PAGE 2: RUNNING BACK ALFRED MORRIS
PAGES 4–5: FULLBACK/RUNNING BACK JOHN RIGGINS
PAGE 6: TACKLE TRENT WILLIAMS

TABLE OF CONTENTS

MONUMENTAL ATTRACTION 8

SUPER BOWL SUCCESS 18

LOOKING FOR A LEADER 26

TRANSITIONS AND TRAGEDIES 34

SIDELINE STORIES

HAIL TO THE REDSKINS 13

LOMBARDI'S LEGACY 17

HOGGING THE GLORY 22

A SUPER QUARTER 25

THE TAYLOR TRAGEDY 36

THE RIVALRY 41

MEET THE REDSKINS

GEORGE PRESTON MARSHALL 10

SAMMY BAUGH 16

JOHN RIGGINS 20

ART MONK 28

JOE GIBBS 32

DARRELL GREEN 45

INDEX 48

WASHINGTON, D.C., IS FAMOUS FOR ITS MONUMENTS AND BUILDINGS

Monumental Attraction

Tourists have plenty of reasons to visit Washington, D.C. As the capital of the United States and the site of many of the country's most historic monuments, the city has long been a favored destination for millions of Americans and visitors from other countries as well. For many of those visitors, exploring Washington's museums, monuments, and governmental buildings brings the history and traditions they represent to life.

But visitors also arrive in Washington eager to participate in an entirely different tradition—one more rooted in sport than in history. Since 1937, the city has been home to a National Football League (NFL) franchise known as the Washington Redskins. The team moved to Washington after five seasons in Boston, Massachusetts, where fans' support for the mediocre team was lackluster. Franchise owner George Preston

REDSKINS 14
WIN - 6

A PROUD MOMENT IN REDSKINS HISTORY WAS THE 1942 NFL CHAMPIONSHIP

George Preston Marshall

TEAM FOUNDER, OWNER / REDSKINS SEASONS: 1932–62

From the time he founded the Redskins until he retired because of poor health, George Preston Marshall controlled every aspect of the franchise. Known as "The Big Chief," Marshall had an opinion on everything that had to do with the Redskins. He would fire coaches in a flash and often send suggestions for plays to his coach during a game. He would even telephone instructions from his private box to the team's band director about what songs to play. The one thing Marshall would not do for many years was sign an African American player for the Redskins. He was finally forced to change his ways in 1962 when the federal government threatened to kick the team out of RFK Stadium if it didn't hire black players. Marshall was a true pioneer of professional football and was part of a committee that created many of the rules that helped the sport grow, including those that permitted more passing and created hash marks for marking the placement of the football on the field. He may have been strong-minded, but his primary aim was always to improve the Redskins.

"SLINGIN' SAMMY" BAUGH BECAME THE FACE OF THE REDSKINS TEAM

Marshall, who owned other businesses in Washington, decided to give his club a fresh start by moving it to the nation's capital.

The 1937 Redskins adopted more than just a new hometown. They also embraced a new look that Marshall hoped would draw more fan attention than the team had received in Boston. When they played their first game in Washington, the Redskins were decked out in new uniforms of gold and burgundy and, more importantly, featured a new star: rookie quarterback Sammy Baugh. Baugh had earned the nickname "Slingin' Sammy" at Texas Christian University because of his skill as a passer. At the time, passing was a far less prominent part of the game—but once Baugh began slinging passes around the field, football was changed forever. As *New York Times* sportswriter Arthur Daley noted, "It was Baugh who revolutionized football and altered all previous offensive strategies."

ith Baugh, offensive end Wayne Millner, and halfback Cliff Battles leading the way, the Redskins topped the NFL's Eastern Division in their first season in Washington. Then they traveled to Chicago to take on the powerful Bears in the NFL Championship Game. Washington's chances looked slim when Baugh, battered by Bears defenders, could barely drag himself into the locker room at halftime. But in the second half, the taped-up quarterback completed two long touchdown passes to Millner to lead the Redskins to a 28–21 win and the team's first NFL title.

Baugh played three major roles for the Redskins during his amazing career. In addition to being the starting quarterback, he was also the team's best defensive back and an outstanding punter. He excelled in all three capacities as he led Washington to a second NFL East title in 1940 and another championship game against Chicago. This time, though, the Bears got their revenge by walloping the Redskins 73–0 in the most lopsided championship game of all time.

That humiliating loss didn't cripple the Redskins or their fans, however. The Redskins drew large crowds to Griffith Stadium in Washington. And, because the team was based farther south than any other franchise in the NFL at the time, it became the "home team" for millions of football fans in Southern states. Those fans were thrilled when Washington topped the NFL East in 1942, 1943, and 1945 and earned a second league title by defeating the Bears in the 1942 championship game.

By the time Slingin' Sammy retired in 1952, he had set almost all of the NFL's passing records, including two (most seasons leading the league in passing, six; and most seasons leading the league with the lowest interception percentage, five) that still stand today. His number 33 jersey is the only one that has ever been officially retired by the Redskins.

Following Baugh's retirement, the Redskins entered a dark period in their history. The team managed to achieve only three winning records throughout the 1950s and '60s. Still, Washington fans loudly cheered the efforts of such standouts as undersized quarterback Eddie LeBaron. The "Little General" stood 5-foot-9 and weighed only 168 pounds, but he thrilled fans with his scrambling maneuvers and ability to pass around and over much bigger defenders. Other fan favorites included two-way stars Gene Brito, who played both offensive and defensive end, and Dick James, the team's top rusher and defensive back.

The Redskins' fortunes began to improve in the mid-1960s, thanks to several strategic moves. In 1962, Washington acquired running back Bobby Mitchell from the Cleveland Browns. Mitchell was the first African American player in the team's history, and he paved the way for other black stars in Washington. An outstanding runner, pass receiver, and kick returner, Mitchell led the NFL in pass receiving his first two seasons in Washington. The Redskins were the last NFL team to sign black players, largely because of the prejudices of their owner, and this sad fact may have been one

Hail to the Redskins

George Preston Marshall was a showman who believed that fans attending a Redskins contest should be entertained before, during, and after a game. So in 1937, the team's first year in Washington, he put together an all-volunteer band to play the fans into and out of the stadium and to put on halftime "extravaganzas." The Washington Redskins Marching Band that Marshall organized was the first of its kind, and its 150 members are still performing at FedExField today. It has also put on special performances for team victory parades, starting with the one honoring the team's first NFL championship in 1937. One year after forming the band, Marshall decided that the club needed its own fight song. Famed dance-band leader Barnee Breeskin, a close friend of Marshall's, composed a spirited melody to go with lyrics written by Marshall's wife Corinne Griffith, a star of 1920s silent films. The song, "Hail to the Redskins," is still first in the hearts of Washington football fans, who loudly proclaim at each game, "Hail to the Redskins! Hail to victory! Braves on the warpath, fight for old D.C."

THE ALL-VOLUNTEER SQUAD IS ONE OF TWO MARCHING BANDS IN PRO FOOTBALL

FUTURE HALL-OF-FAMER SONNY JURGENSEN ATTENDED 5 PRO BOWLS BEFORE 1970

reason that other teams
outperformed the Redskins
during the 1950s and '60s.

Washington's management
made two other key moves
in 1964, trading with the
Philadelphia Eagles for
quarterback Sonny Jurgensen
and with the New York Giants
for linebacker Sam Huff.
Jurgensen—known for his
strong arm, slow feet, and
tremendous confidence—
revived memories of Sammy
Baugh in Washington fans.
He teamed with Mitchell
and rookie wide receiver
Charley Taylor to turn the
sluggish Redskins offense
into a highflying aerial
attack. Huff, who had helped
lead the Giants to six NFL
Championship Games,
brought an intensity to the
Redskins' defense that had
been missing. His philosophy
of the game was very simple:
"Get the man with the
football!" he would shout at
his teammates.

Sammy Baugh

QUARTERBACK / REDSKINS SEASONS: 1937–52 / HEIGHT: 6-FOOT-2 / WEIGHT: 180 POUNDS

"Slingin' Sammy" Baugh was one of pro football's first great passers. Born in Texas farming country, Baugh first made headlines as a football and baseball star at Texas Christian University. Redskins owner George Preston Marshall decided Baugh was the ideal player to win over fans in Washington, where the team would be moving in 1937. To convince Baugh to sign with the Redskins instead of with baseball's St. Louis Cardinals, Marshall raised his salary offer to a lofty $8,000. The big contract turned out to be a bargain. At Baugh's first training camp, his new coach, Ray Flaherty, put him through some tough passing drills. Flaherty marked a spot on the field and said, "When the receiver reaches this spot, I want you to hit him in the eye with the ball." Baugh quickly responded, "Which eye?" For the next 15 years, Baugh impressed both coaches and fans with his passing accuracy and his toughness. He led the NFL in passing six times and, in 1963, was in the first class of players inducted into the Pro Football Hall of Fame.

Lombardi's Legacy

Vince Lombardi is best known for building the Green Bay Packers into one of the NFL's most impressive dynasties in the 1960s. But the year he spent in Washington—1969—may have been the greatest tribute to his legacy as a winner. In that one season, he helped transform the Redskins from a bumbling, sub-.500 franchise that hadn't posted a winning season in 13 years into an NFL powerhouse for the next 2 decades. Lombardi made several key on-field changes. First, he opened up the team's offense, helping quarterback Sonny Jurgensen and receiver Charley Taylor become the most fearsome tandem in the league. Then he made rookie Larry Brown, an unheralded eighth-round draft pick, his primary running back. Brown would lead the Redskins in rushing for six straight seasons. Even more important were the changes Lombardi made inside his players. "Lombardi was able to get inside your heart and mind and lead you to levels way above your abilities and skills," said guard Vince Promuto. Suddenly, there was a winning atmosphere in Washington's RFK Stadium that would last long after Lombardi's untimely death.

VINCE LOMBARDI WAS A HANDS-ON COACH WHEN IT CAME TO PRACTICE

Super Bowl Success

Although the additions of Jurgensen and Huff revitalized the Redskins, Washington didn't become a winner again until 1969, when Hall of Fame coach Vince Lombardi came out of retirement to lead the team. Before the 1969 season opener, Lombardi reminded his new players that he had never coached a losing club. "And nothing is going to change that," he insisted.

Inspired by their coach's confidence, the Redskins finally broke their losing streak with a 7–5–2 record in 1969. Spirits were high in Washington, but they soon fell again. During the off-season, Coach Lombardi died suddenly from cancer. The Redskins reverted to their losing ways in 1970, but they were ready for a major turnaround when George Allen took the reins the following year.

Allen, a big winner as coach of the Los Angeles Rams, didn't want to take the time to

THE REDSKINS REACHED SUPER BOWL XVII AFTER A 10-YEAR ABSENCE FROM THE BIG GAME

✕John Riggins

**RUNNING BACK / REDSKINS SEASONS: 1976–79, 1981–85 /
HEIGHT: 6-FOOT-2 / WEIGHT: 230 POUNDS**

Ask Redskins fans to name the most famous play in franchise history, and they'll likely reply, "John Riggins's game-winning, 43-yard touchdown run in Super Bowl XVII." That touchdown jaunt was just one of many outstanding runs that Riggins made during his career in Washington. He still holds team career records for most rushing attempts, rushing yards, and rushing touchdowns. Riggins possessed an unusual combination of power, speed, and cockiness. He was also a little crazy. He once came into training camp sporting a Mohawk haircut. Another year, he showed up wearing only shorts and a derby hat with a feather in it. Riggins started his pro career with the New York Jets and then signed with the Redskins in 1976. He left the team before the 1980 season over a contract dispute but returned one year later after a meeting with new coach Joe Gibbs. "I'm bored, I'm broke, and I'm back," he announced to fans before resuming his record-breaking career. In 1992, Riggins was inducted into the Pro Football Hall of Fame.

"I'm bored, I'm broke, and I'm back."

JOHN RIGGINS AFTER A CONTRACT DISPUTE

develop young talent in Washington. Instead, he immediately began trading away future draft choices for established stars. Among the veterans who arrived in Washington were quarterback Billy Kilmer, linebacker Jack Pardee, and safety Richie Petitbon, all of whom were in their 30s. Fans and writers soon began calling the Redskins the "Over the Hill Gang."

Allen's gamble paid off, though. The Over the Hill Gang made the playoffs in 1971 after posting a 9–4–1 record. It was the club's first postseason appearance in 25 years. The next year, the Redskins captured the National Football Conference (NFC) championship and earned the club's first Super Bowl berth, only to fall to the undefeated Miami Dolphins in the championship game, 14–7.

Coach Allen's Redskins made the playoffs three more times from 1973 to 1977 but failed to reach the Super Bowl again. In 1978, Allen was replaced by now retired player Jack Pardee, who promoted backup quarterback Joe Theismann to the starting role. "You've paid your dues," Pardee told his new passer. "Now it's time to take charge and get this team rolling again. The future is now."

While Jurgensen and Kilmer had been strictly drop-back passers, Theismann loved to scramble to keep opposing defensive linemen off balance. Joining Theismann in the backfield was running back John Riggins, whom teammates called "The Diesel" because he roared through the line like a powerful truck. In 1980, the Redskins added another future offensive star by drafting young receiver Art Monk out of Syracuse University.

Despite their offensive improvements, the Redskins remained a middle-of-the-pack team until Joe Gibbs took over as coach in 1981. Gibbs rebuilt the team's defense around nose guard Dave Butz and ends Dexter Manley and Charles Mann. To the offensive line he added several huge blockers, known affectionately as "The Hogs." Gibbs's Redskins quickly rose to the top of the NFC and reached the Super Bowl in the coach's second season at the helm.

In January 1983, exactly 10 years after their first Super Bowl appearance, the Redskins faced off against the Dolphins once again for the NFL championship. This time the result would be different.

Hogging the Glory

When most fans think about the 1983 Super Bowl, they recall John Riggins's game-breaking touchdown run. What they don't always remember is who opened up the huge hole in the Miami Dolphins' defense through which Riggins ran. Those players were 300-pound tackle Joe Jacoby and 275-pound guard Russ Grimm, and they were charter members of one of the most famous offensive lines of all time—"The Hogs." The Hogs got their nickname from the team's offensive coordinator, Joe Bugel. "A Hog," Bugel explained, "is a guy who gets down and does a dirty job without wanting to be beautiful." In the 1980s, the tackles, guards, centers, and tight ends who made up The Hogs became almost as well known in Washington as the team's backs and receivers. Many Redskins fans showed up at RFK Stadium each week wearing hog noses, hog hats, or hog T-shirts to show their love for their hardworking heroes. The Hogs also included one player who didn't toil on the offensive line—Riggins. He was admitted because "he has the personality of a Hog," said veteran tight end George Starke.

THE HOGS INSPIRED FANS TO DRESS IN PIGGISH COSTUMES AS "THE HOGETTES"

BEFORE JOINING THE REDSKINS, JOE THEISMANN PLAYED IN THE CANADIAN PROS

Theismann played brilliantly, tossing two touchdown passes. But his most important move was handing the ball off to Riggins on a fourth-down play early in the fourth quarter. Miami was ahead 17–13, and everyone was expecting Riggins to simply dive forward a yard for the first down. Instead, The Diesel slid toward his left, broke through the tightly packed defenders, and raced 43 yards for a touchdown that sealed the Redskins' first Super Bowl triumph.

ashington was even more dominant the next year, breaking several league scoring records en route to a 14–2 season. The team reached the Super Bowl once again but fell to the Los Angeles Raiders, 38–9, failing to win a second consecutive title. Still, many Redskins players and fans believed that the 1983 club was the franchise's best ever. "We were the best team in the history of Washington football," said Theismann, who was named the league's Most Valuable Player (MVP) in

1983. "But that will never be known because we didn't win a Super Bowl."

By 1987, a new lineup was in place in Washington. Theismann and Riggins had both retired and been replaced by quarterback Doug Williams and running back George Rogers. The Redskins dominated the NFC East Division with an 11–4 record during the regular season. In the postseason, Williams led Washington to victories over the Chicago Bears and Minnesota Vikings and into another Super Bowl.

Facing the Denver Broncos in the Super Bowl, the Redskins quickly fell behind 10–0. Then Williams let his strong right arm take over, tossing a Super Bowl–record four second-quarter touchdown passes to spark an amazing turnaround. The Redskins went on to win 42–10, and Williams was named the game's MVP. Afterwards, Williams was asked about the remarkable comeback. "It was destined," he said simply. "It was in the cards."

After suffering a back injury the next season, Williams was replaced by big (6-foot-4 and 230 pounds) and tough quarterback Mark Rypien. The young passer led the club to winning seasons in 1989, 1990, and 1991. Then, in the 1991 playoffs, Rypien earned his own Super Bowl MVP award when he guided the Redskins to a decisive 37–24 championship victory over the Buffalo Bills.

A Super Quarter

Doug Williams had a brief career as a Redskins quarterback, but the one nearly perfect quarter he played during Super Bowl XXII on January 31, 1988, forever earned him an honored place in the team's history. "We scored 35 points in 18 plays—that's execution at its very best," recalled Williams. "Offensively, we were in a zone. It didn't matter who we were playing; they weren't going to stop us." The five-touchdown outburst by the Redskins in the second quarter of the game turned a 10–0 Denver Broncos lead into a 35–10 Washington rout. From there, the 'Skins coasted to a 42–10 victory. Amazingly, Williams nearly missed out on this historic quarter. Near the end of the first period, he hyperextended his left knee and limped off the field. He was back for the Redskins' next offensive series, however, and the fireworks began. Starting with a Super Bowl–record 80-yard touchdown pass to wide receiver Ricky Sanders, Williams completed 18 of 29 passes during the game for 340 yards and 4 touchdowns. "Doug was the right man in the right place," said coach Joe Gibbs.

DOUG WILLIAMS HAD HIS BEST SEASON WITH THE 'SKINS IN 1988

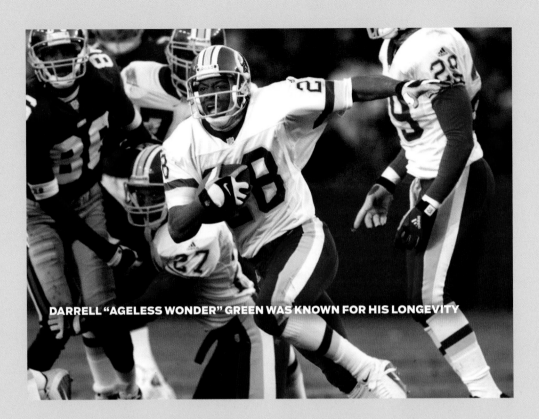

DARRELL "AGELESS WONDER" GREEN WAS KNOWN FOR HIS LONGEVITY

Looking for a Leader

Coach Gibbs spent one more season directing the Redskins before retiring in 1993. He left as the most successful coach in franchise history, having reached the playoffs eight times and appeared in four Super Bowls, winning three of them. Gibbs's departure was followed by a decline in the team's fortunes. The Redskins dropped to the middle of the NFC East standings under coaches Richie Petitbon and Norv Turner and didn't reach the playoffs again until 1999, despite the heroics of such players as running back Terry Allen, kick returner Brian Mitchell, and cornerback Darrell Green.

Before the 1999 season, the Redskins made a key addition, drafting cornerback Champ Bailey out of the University of Georgia. With a defense featuring Bailey and an offense led by quarterback Brad Johnson and running back Stephen Davis, the Redskins went 10–6 in 1999. They thrilled the fans who packed FedExField (the team's home since 1997) with several stirring comebacks and came within one point of reaching the NFC Championship Game that year. "We didn't have a lot of big names on the team,"

STEPHEN DAVIS SCORED THE MOST TOUCHDOWNS (17) OF ANY NFL PLAYER IN 1999

Art Monk

WIDE RECEIVER / REDSKINS SEASONS: 1980–93 / HEIGHT: 6-FOOT-3 / WEIGHT: 210 POUNDS

On October 13, 1992, Art Monk caught his 820th pass to become the NFL's all-time leader in pass receptions. (Monk's record has since been broken by 11 other players.) That record-breaking catch was a tribute both to Monk's skill as a receiver and his remarkable consistency. From his rookie season in 1980 until he left Washington in 1993, Monk caught 50 or more passes 9 times and topped the 100 mark in 1984. "Art was quiet about his work but very loud with his results," said Washington quarterback Mark Rypien. Added Redskins general manager Charley Casserly, "There was never a classier player in the franchise's history, or in league history, than Art Monk. You always knew the team would be getting Art Monk's best effort day in and day out." Monk was the team's top draft choice out of New York's Syracuse University in 1980 and quickly became a star, winning the award as the NFL's top offensive rookie that year. Monk was a dominant receiver throughout the 1980s and was voted to the Pro Bowl three times during the decade.

DEION SANDERS WAS NOT IN HIS PRIME DURING HIS 1999 SEASON WITH THE 'SKINS

recalled linebacker Eddie Mason. "We had a bunch of guys who played well together and were tight like a family. We knew how to win and come together. That is what it takes."

Unfortunately, the excitement of 1999 soon faded in the new century, and the club's new owner, 35-year-old billionaire Daniel Snyder, quickly became impatient. Using the same daring tactics that had helped him achieve success in business, Snyder made a number of expensive but misguided decisions. He spent millions of dollars bringing in veteran stars such as defensive end Bruce Smith, cornerback Deion Sanders, and quarterback Jeff George to recharge the team. But instead of improving the squad, those additions seemed to destroy the chemistry that had helped the 1999 team succeed.

Snyder also made rash decisions about coaches. After the 'Skins slumped at the end of the 2000 season, he fired Turner and replaced him with veteran coach Marty Schottenheimer. When Schottenheimer's club went a mere 8–8 in his first year, Snyder decided to bring in college "supercoach" Steve Spurrier to take over the Redskins.

Spurrier, a former NFL quarterback who had won the 1996 college national championship as coach of the Florida Gators, was thrilled with the challenge and predicted a bright future for the Redskins. "We're going to turn FedExField into the loudest stadium in the country," he said. Unfortunately, much of the noise that Spurrier heard in the Redskins' stadium over the next two years consisted of boos. Despite

the additions of strong-armed quarterback Patrick Ramsey and wide receiver Laveranues Coles to enhance the offense and the presence of All-Pro defenders such as Bailey and linebacker LaVar Arrington, Spurrier's teams suffered through losing seasons in both 2002 and 2003 before the coach resigned and returned to the college ranks.

Faced with making a fourth coaching change in only five years, Snyder decided that only one man possessed the right combination of football savvy, coaching style, and a history of success needed to return the Redskins to their former glory—Joe Gibbs. So, on January 9, 2004, Snyder surprised the sports world by announcing that Gibbs would be coming back to Washington after an 11-year absence. Appearing at a press conference that day, Gibbs told reporters that he purposely was not wearing any of the Super Bowl rings

COACH SPURRIER'S FIRST CAMPAIGN IN WASHINGTON WAS STEPHEN DAVIS'S LAST

✕Joe Gibbs

COACH / REDSKINS SEASONS: 1981–92, 2004–07

During the 1970s, the Redskins were a solid but predictable team. That began to change when Joe Gibbs was hired as coach in 1981. Gibbs had built a reputation for being an offensive genius as an assistant coach with the San Diego Chargers. Upon arriving in Washington, he immediately began shaking things up. Gibbs drafted several outstanding young offensive linemen to block for his quarterback, convinced running back John Riggins to abandon retirement and return to the team, and began transforming the Redskins from a "grind-it-out" club into one that continually surprised opposing defenders by slashing through or passing over them. "Gibbs is a man of perception and a coach of deception," said one Washington sportswriter. In his second year in Washington, Gibbs led the Redskins to their first Super Bowl triumph. The 'Skins would play in three more Super Bowls and win two more championships before Gibbs retired in 1992 to focus on his other main interest—directing a successful team of race-car drivers. Gibbs came out of retirement in 2004 and led the Redskins back to the playoffs one year later.

CHRIS COOLEY HELD THE TEAM'S RECORD FOR MOST RECEPTIONS AT TIGHT END

that he had earned in his earlier stint with the Redskins. "We're focused on the future," he said. "I love the challenge of doing something that's almost undoable."

Facing his new challenge head-on, Gibbs began making significant changes. He engineered a trade of All-Pro players with the Broncos, sending Bailey to Denver in exchange for running back Clinton Portis, whose straight-ahead running style reminded older Washington fans of John Riggins. Gibbs also signed free-agent quarterback Mark Brunell to direct the offense.

Despite those solid additions to the roster, the 'Skins averaged fewer than 20 points per game in 2004 and finished with a dismal 6–10 record. Even after trading for speedy wide receiver Santana Moss, they got off to a rocky start in 2005 as well, and fans worried that the team might suffer two straight losing seasons for the first time ever under Gibbs. Then the Redskins rebounded, winning their last five games and roaring into the playoffs with a 10–6 record.

They continued their winning ways in the postseason against the Tampa Bay Buccaneers. Led by defensive standouts such as linebacker Marcus Washington and safety Sean Taylor, the Redskins hounded Tampa Bay quarterback Chris Simms all afternoon on their way to a 17–10 win. The defense remained strong in the team's next playoff game against the Seattle Seahawks, but the offense sputtered. The result was a 20–10, season-ending loss. "We hit a rough point this year when we were 5–6, and guys could have pointed fingers," said Portis. "But nobody did. We won a tough one last week and lost a tough one this week. We've got more to look forward to next year."

IN 2007, MIKE SELLERS (#45) CONTRIBUTED THREE TOUCHDOWNS

Transitions and Tragedies

Unfortunately, 2006 turned out to be a year that most Redskins fans wanted to forget. Portis was injured for much of the season, and Brunell proved to be inconsistent under center. By November, when the veteran quarterback had found the end zone only eight times in the first nine games, Gibbs decided to replace his veteran signal-caller with second-year quarterback Jason Campbell, who had been an All-American at Auburn University in Alabama. Although Campbell posted respectable numbers during his 7 games as a starter, including tossing the first 10 touchdown passes of his career, the season ended with a disappointing 5–11 record.

Fans who had braced themselves for a repeat the following season were pleasantly surprised when Washington won five of its first eight games in 2007. Led by a rapidly maturing Campbell, along with a recovered Portis, Moss, and tight end Chris Cooley,

CLINTON PORTIS RACKED UP 8,164 TOTAL YARDS IN 7 SEASONS WITH THE REDSKINS

The Taylor Tragedy

Sean Taylor didn't suit up for the Washington Redskins' game against the Tampa Bay Buccaneers on November 25, 2007. The 24-year-old safety was injured and couldn't play, so he drove to his home in Miami to spend the weekend with his girlfriend and their daughter. While he was there, an intruder broke into his home and shot him. When Taylor died a day later, both his teammates and fans were shocked and saddened. Fans laid flowers, cards, and other mementos near the front entrance to Redskins Park; some stood silently in the empty parking space that had been given to Taylor when he was honored as the team's defensive player of the week earlier in the season. The Redskins honored him with a service before playing the Buffalo Bills on December 2 at FedExField. The next day, the entire team left Washington to travel together to Miami for Taylor's funeral. They were among 3,000 people who gathered to say goodbye to the football player. "What got cut short here was a career that was going to go to a lot of Pro Bowls and have a lot of fun," Redskins coach Joe Gibbs said.

the 'Skins seemed to be headed for the playoffs by midseason. Then they lost three tight contests in a row and appeared to be in a free fall instead.

Things turned from terrible to tragic in early December 2007, when All-Pro safety Sean Taylor was shot to death by burglars in his Miami home. Gibbs gathered his players together and tried to console them. "Sometimes in life, maybe some of the best things happen to you after you have been kind of crushed," he said. He hoped the team would come together over the next few weeks, both to grieve for their teammate and to finish the season in a way that would honor Taylor's memory. The 'Skins made a heroic comeback, winning their last four contests and earning a Wild Card berth in

PRO-BOWLER PORTIS WAS PLAGUED BY INJURIES IN HIS FINAL SEASONS

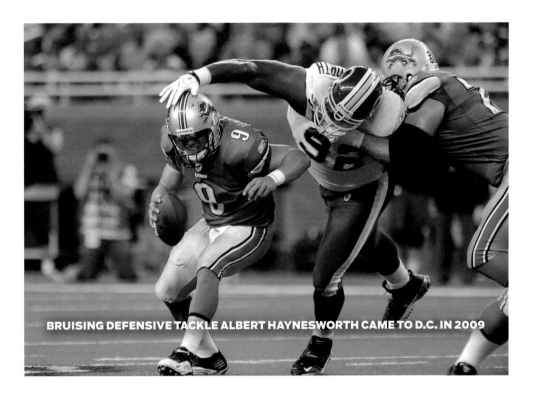
BRUISING DEFENSIVE TACKLE ALBERT HAYNESWORTH CAME TO D.C. IN 2009

the postseason before falling to the Seahawks in the first round of the playoffs.

Two days after losing to Seattle, the 67-year-old Gibbs surprised his players and the Washington fans by announcing that he would once again be retiring as head coach so that he could spend more time with his family—including his grandson, who had recently been diagnosed with leukemia. "My family situation being what it is right now, I told [Snyder] I couldn't make the kind of commitment I needed to make," Gibbs told reporters. "I felt like [my family] needed me."

Under new head coach Jim Zorn, who had started his NFL career quarterbacking for the Seahawks, and behind the offensive leadership of Campbell, Washington began the 2008 season by winning four of its first five games and staying close to the top of the pack in the NFC East. But then came December. Not only did the Redskins lose three of the four games they played that month, but they also received word that Sammy Baugh, whose heroics had helped build the franchise, had died at the age of 94. Although their 8–8 record was respectable, there was a deep sense of loss within the organization as the season ended.

Washington remained in a funk for all of 2009 as well. Both Portis and Moss underperformed, amassing only five touchdowns between them. Linebacker Brian Orakpo and defensive end Andre Carter provided most of the team's highlights, as both of them notched 11 quarterback sacks during a miserable

The Rivalry

When the Redskins defeated the Dallas Cowboys in the final game of the 2007 season to complete their remarkable turnaround to reach the playoffs, it marked another highlight in perhaps the greatest rivalry in professional football. The Redskins and Cowboys have been playing hard-fought games ever since Dallas entered the NFL in 1960. In fact, Washington's only win in 1960 came against the expansion Cowboys. Since the two teams have always been in the same NFC division, they have played each other at least twice a year—more than 100 times in all. The Cowboys hold the edge in total victories in the series, but the Redskins have won two of the most important games, topping Dallas in the NFC Championship Game in both 1972 and 1982 on their way to their first two Super Bowl appearances. Other key Washington victories included late-season, playoff-clinching wins in 1976 and 1984. "It's the Redskins versus the Cowboys; it doesn't get much better than that," said famed television commentator John Madden before a battle between the rivals in the 2000s. "It just sounds like football."

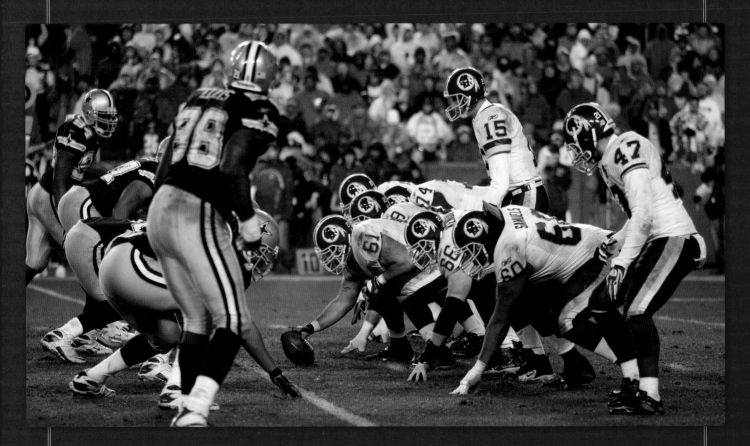

AS OF 2013, THE TWO RIVALS HAD AMASSED EIGHT SUPER BOWL WINS BETWEEN THEM

BACK CHRIS HORTON (#48) AND WIDE RECEIVER ANTWAAN RANDLE EL (#82)

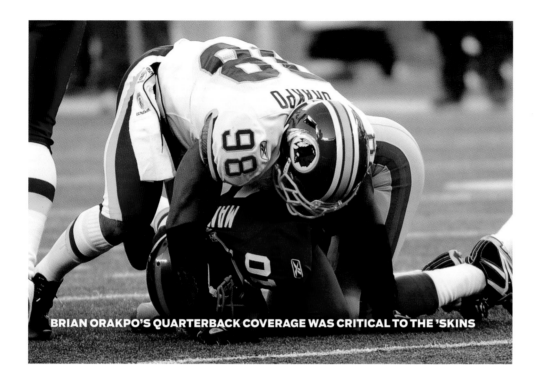

BRIAN ORAKPO'S QUARTERBACK COVERAGE WAS CRITICAL TO THE 'SKINS

4–12 season. Zorn, who had compiled a 12–20 record during his two-year tenure with the team, was then released. "No one in the organization is satisfied with our record over the last two years," team owner Daniel Snyder said. "I am sure that Jim would concur with that statement. It has been painful for him, too. I certainly accept responsibility for mistakes that I have made."

To help make up for those mistakes, Snyder hired former Broncos coach Mike Shanahan, who had taken Denver to 2 Super Bowl championships during his 14 years with the team. Then Snyder brought in quarterback Donovan McNabb, who had led the rival Philadelphia Eagles to the Super Bowl in 2004. Although McNabb was supposed to have been the star of the show in 2010, the aging quarterback was upstaged by cornerback DeAngelo Hall. Hall helped the Redskins beat the Cowboys in the first game of the season by forcing a fumble and returning it 32 yards for a touchdown. He also intercepted four passes in a close 17–14 win over the Bears in October. Hall's stellar play was rewarded with a trip to the Pro Bowl at the end of the season.

But there were no postseason trips for the rest of the Redskins in either 2010 or 2011. Although the defense remained strong behind Orakpo and rookie linebacker Ryan Kerrigan, McNabb's departure contributed to a lackluster offensive effort, and both seasons ended with losing records. The team tried to improve its chances before the 2012 season by looking for a quarterback to turn Washington into a winner again.

Darrell Green

CORNERBACK / REDSKINS SEASONS: 1983–2002 / HEIGHT: 5-FOOT-8 / WEIGHT: 185 POUNDS

When Darrell Green first joined the Redskins in 1983, he was known primarily for his speed, as he could run the 40-yard dash in a remarkable 4.13 seconds. His skill as a cornerback soon shone through, too. During a playoff game against the Los Angeles Rams, the rookie intercepted a pass and returned it 72 yards for a touchdown to help seal a Washington victory. Green played 19 more seasons with the Redskins and barely slowed down at all. By the time he retired in 2002, he held the club record for most interceptions, which still stands today; he also set records for most interceptions returned for touchdowns, most games played, and most games started. "He had great, great feet and switched directions so well," said Dallas Cowboys receiver Alvin Harper, who battled Green for many years. "If you faked one way, and he closed that way, and then you went another way, he would whirl around so fast it was like he was on the same path with you the whole time." A seven-time Pro-Bowler, Green was also named NFL Man of the Year in 1996 for his charitable work in the Washington area and was inducted into the Hall of Fame in 2008.

ROOKIE SENSATION ROBERT GRIFFIN III PASSED FOR 20 TOUCHDOWNS IN 2012

END STEPHEN BOWEN ADDED MUSCLE TO WASHINGTON'S DEFENSE

The Redskins found the right man for the job in rookie Robert Griffin III. Popularly known as "RGIII," the quarterback lived up to the hype generated prior to the 2012 NFL Draft and led his new team to a division-clinching, 10–6 season. In Week 11, he became the youngest player in NFL history to achieve a perfect passer rating in a game during a win against the Eagles. Griffin's highlight-reel style of play was fully displayed on Thanksgiving Day, when he threw for 311 yards and 4 touchdowns to help the Redskins defeat archrival Dallas. A knee injury sustained in Week 14 was re-aggravated in the Redskins' Wild Card playoff loss to the Seahawks in January 2013, and Griffin underwent surgery three days later. As Griffin accepted his award for Offensive Rookie of the Year following the season, he assured reporters (and nervous fans) that, after his rehabilitation, he would be back with a vengeance in 2013. "I vowed to my teammates and myself that I would be a different player," he said. "You won't see the same Robert Griffin. You'll see a better Robert Griffin."

The Redskins have been part of the history of Washington, D.C., for more than 70 years. During that span, they've won five championships and developed some of the greatest football players of all time. Although they've suffered through losing seasons as well, Redskins fans trust the tradition their team has built. They know that it won't be long before their team makes Washington the football capital of the U.S. once again.

INDEX

Allen, George 18, 21

Allen, Terry 26

Arrington, LaVar 30

Bailey, Champ 26, 30, 33

Battles, Cliff 11

Baugh, Sammy 11, 12, 15, 16, 40

Boston Redskins 8

Brito, Gene 12

Brown, Larry 17

Brunell, Mark 33, 34

Bugel, Joe 22

Butz, Dave 21

Campbell, Jason 34, 40

Carter, Andre 40

Casserly, Charley 28

Coles, Laveranues 30

Cooley, Chris 34

Davis, Stephen 26

division championships 11, 12, 24, 47

FedExField 13, 26, 29, 36

first season 11

Flaherty, Ray 16

George, Jeff 29

Gibbs, Joe 21, 25, 26, 30, 32, 33, 34, 36, 37, 40

Green, Darrell 26, 45

Griffin, Robert III 47

Griffith Stadium 12

Grimm, Russ 22

"Hail to the Redskins" fight song 13

Hall, DeAngelo 44

"The Hogs" offensive line 21, 22

Huff, Sam 15, 18

Jacoby, Joe 22

James, Dick 12

Johnson, Brad 26

Jurgensen, Sonny 15, 17, 18, 21

Kerrigan, Ryan 44

Kilmer, Billy 21

LeBaron, Eddie 12

Lombardi, Vince 17, 18

Man of the Year award 45

Manley, Dexter 21

Mann, Charles 21

Marshall, George Preston 8, 10, 11, 13, 16

Mason, Eddie 29

McNabb, Donovan 44

Millner, Wayne 11

Mitchell, Bobby 12

Mitchell, Brian 26

Monk, Art 21, 28

Moss, Santana 33, 34, 40

MVP award 23, 24

NFC Championship Game 26, 41

NFC championships 21

NFL Championship Game 11, 12

NFL championships 11, 12, 13, 47

NFL records 12, 23, 28, 47

Offensive Rookie of the Year award 28, 47

Orakpo, Brian 40, 44

"Over the Hill Gang" 21

Pardee, Jack 21

Petitbon, Richie 21, 26

playoffs 21, 24, 26, 32, 33, 40, 41, 45, 47

Portis, Clinton 33, 34, 40

Pro Bowl 28, 44, 45

Pro Football Hall of Fame 16, 20, 45

Promuto, Vince 17

Ramsey, Patrick 30

retired numbers 12

RFK Stadium 10, 17, 22

Riggins, John 20, 21, 22, 23, 24, 32, 33

rivalry with Dallas Cowboys 41, 47

Rogers, George 24

Rypien, Mark 24, 28

Sanders, Deion 29

Sanders, Ricky 25

Schottenheimer, Marty 29

Shanahan, Mike 44

Smith, Bruce 29

Snyder, Daniel 29, 30, 40, 44

Spurrier, Steve 29, 30

Starke, George 22

Super Bowl 20, 21, 22, 23, 24, 25, 26, 32, 41

Super Bowl records 24, 25

Taylor, Charley 15, 17

Taylor, Sean 33, 36, 37

team band 10, 13

team records 20, 45

Theismann, Joe 21, 23, 24

Turner, Norv 26, 29

Washington, Marcus 33

Williams, Doug 24, 25

Zorn, Jim 40, 44